50
fantastic things to do with
Toddlers

SALLY AND PHILL FEATHERSTONE

Contents

Published 2010 by A&C Black Publishers Limited
36 Soho Square, London, W1D 3QY
www.acblack.com

ISBN 978-1-4081-2324-9

Copyright © A&C Black Publishers Ltd 2010

Written by Sally Featherstone and Phill Featherstone
Design by Bob Vickers
Photographs © Shutterstock 2010

Printed in Great Britain by Latimer Trend & Company Limited

A CIP record for this publication is available from the British Library.

The right of the authors to be identified as the authors of this work has been asserted in accordance with Sections 77 and 78 of the Copyright, Designs and Patents Act, 1988.

This book is produced using paper that is made from wood grown in managed, sustainable forests. It is natural, renewable and recyclable. The logging and manufacturing processes conform to the environmental regulations of the country of origin.

To see our full range of titles
Visit www.acblack.com/featherstone

Introduction

There's plenty of research to show that babies and children who enjoy a stimulating home environment learn better and more quickly. So what parents and carers do to lay the groundwork for learning early on is an investment that pays back throughout their child's life.

This book has been specially written for parents to use with their young children at home. However, it can also be used by carers and workers in nurseries and childcare settings. It contains 50 simple activities that can be done easily with very little equipment, often in odd moments of time. It's not a course to work through. All the ideas here are suitable for babies from 16–36 months, and in many cases beyond. Some are more suited to younger babies and some to older. It's obvious which these are. Choose what you and your child enjoy. When you find an activity you like, do it again, and again, and again. Babies love repetition and benefit from it.

There are four books in the 50 Fantastic Things series:

50 Fantastic Things to Do With Babies (suitable for use from soon after birth to 20 months)

50 Fantastic Things to Do With Toddlers (suitable for use from 16–36 months)

50 Fantastic Things to Do With Pre-Schoolers (suitable for use from 30–50 months)

50 Fantastic Things to Do With Four and Five Year Olds (suitable for use from 40–60+ months)

The age groupings above are approximate and are only suggestions. Children develop at different speeds. They also grow in spurts, with some periods of rapid development alternating with other times when they don't seem to change as quickly. So don't worry if your baby doesn't seem ready for a particular activity. Try another instead and return to it later. On the other hand, if your baby gets on well and quickly, try some of the ideas in the 'Another idea' and 'Ready for more?' sections.

Finally, please remember that one of the main aims of this book is fun. There are few things as delightful or rewarding as being alongside young children as they explore, enquire, experiment and learn. Join them in their enthusiasm for learning, and enjoy being with them!

A NOTE ON SAFETY

Care must be taken at all times when dealing with babies and young children. Common sense will be your main guide, but here are a few ideas to help you have fun safely.

Babies and young children naturally explore things by bringing them to their mouths. This is fine, but always check that toys and other objects you use are clean.

Although rare, swallowing objects or choking on them are hazards. Some children are more susceptible than others. If you are concerned about choking, buy a choke measure from a high street baby shop.

Baby's lungs are delicate. They need clean air. *Never* smoke near your baby, and don't allow anyone else to do so.

Children are naturally inquisitive and you will want to encourage this. However, secure and happy children are often unaware of danger. Your baby needs you to watch out for them. Make sure you are always there. You can't watch your baby all the time, but don't leave him/her alone and unsupervised for more than a few minutes at a time. Even when they are asleep check on them regularly.

The objects and toys we suggest here have been chosen for their safety. Nevertheless, most things can be dangerous if they go wrong or are not used properly:

- Mobiles and toys tied to baby gyms are great to encourage looking and reaching, but check that they are fastened securely.
- Ribbons and string are fascinating to babies but can be a choking hazard. They can also become wrapped round arms, legs and necks.
- Babies are natural explorers. They need clean floors. Store outdoor shoes away from areas where your baby will be lying and crawling.
- If your baby is just learning to balance, either sitting or standing, make sure they have a soft landing. Put a pillow behind babies who are starting to sit. If your baby is starting to crawl or walk, look out for trip hazards.
- Take care with furniture. Make sure your baby is fastened securely into his/her high chair. Pad sharp edges of tables and other furniture.

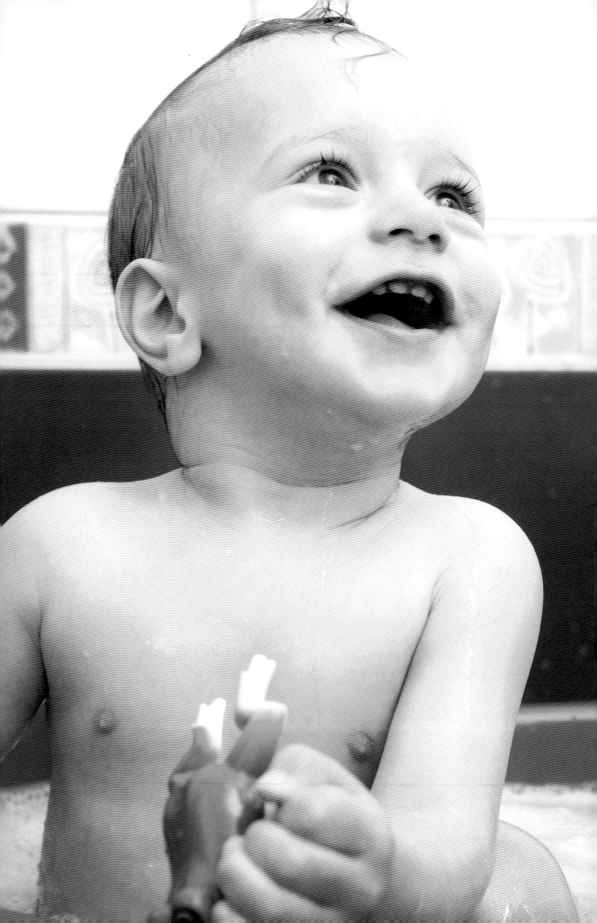

Over to you
giving and taking

What is your child learning?

This is important both for learning to identify objects and naming them, and for developing the concept of sharing.

What you need:

- a basket of everyday objects (e.g. a brush, a sponge, a plastic cup, a wooden spoon, a rattle)

WHAT TO DO:

1. Make sure your baby is sitting comfortably and well supported. Sit opposite them.

2. Put the basket between you and together have a good look at all the objects.

3. Take one of the objects and offer it to your baby. Talk while you do so, and be sure to name the object, e.g. 'Here you are, here's a spoon. Can you take it?'

4. Encourage your baby to take the object from you.

5. Ask him/her to give it back to you, e.g. 'Can you give me the spoon?' Reward with praise and smiles if they do, but don't worry if they want to hang on to it.

Another idea: Play this game at bath time with bath toys.

Ready for more?

If your baby seems ready to move on, ask them to give you a particular thing. Name the object and keep prompting until they pick it up.

Carry on in this way. Don't worry if they don't always give you the thing you name, just take what they give you, name it and thank them!

Don't move on to this until you are sure your baby is ready. If they don't get it, try again a few weeks later.

DID YOU KNOW?

Interactions with other people stimulate brain growth in young children and this helps learning.

It's your choice
learning to point

DID YOU KNOW?
Research tells us that children learn to decode facial expressions and gestures before understanding language.

What you need:
- three small boxes with lids (shoe boxes are ideal)
- three small soft toys

WHAT TO DO:

1. Place a soft toy in each box. Put the lids on and put the boxes on the floor. Sit down with your baby.

2. Show them the boxes. Shake each one to grab their attention. Invite them to choose a box. As they reach towards a box say, 'This one. You want this one?' As you say this make a clear pointing gesture.

3. Open the box together and say the name of the toy it contains.

4. Hug the soft toy and play together, e.g. give teddy a drink, brush the monkey's hair.

5. If your baby is just starting to point, gently take their hand to help them point to and touch the box of their choice.

6. Explore all the boxes, encouraging your baby to use pointing to show choices.

Ready for more?

Play a memory game with the boxes. Ask 'Where's teddy?' and encourage your baby to point to the box where they think it is.

Put a picture in each box. Talk about the pictures and then ask your baby to point to, e.g. the cat, the house, etc.

Another idea: Put a hat, a glove and a shoe in the boxes. Put on the one that's chosen.

What is your child learning?

Gesture is a key way of making yourself understood and pointing is important. This activity develops the use of gesture and helps with linking language to body signals. It also leads to making choices and communicating them.

HELPFUL HINTS

Some children find pointing difficult. Be patient and help by guiding the hand. If your baby goes to a child minder or nursery tell them that you're working on pointing.

If your child loses concentration, hide some bright interesting toys in the boxes.

DID YOU KNOW?

If brain cells are not linked up and strengthened at an early age these connections may not form at all.

Squeezy peasy
using hands to explore

What you need:
- a shallow bowl, a board or small tray
- squidgy stuff – e.g. dough, pastry mix, or cooked pasta mixed with a little oil

WHAT TO DO:

1. Mix the dough or cook the pasta where your child can see, hear and smell what you are doing. Leave cooked items to cool.

2. Put some of the squidgy stuff between you on the board or tray or in the bowl.

3. Encourage your child to reach out and grab some of the stuff with both hands. Join in the fun!

4. Talk about how it feels as you squeeze the stuff in your hands and between your fingers. Use words like 'squidgy', 'slimy', 'squashy'.

A baby or younger child may bring the stuff towards their face. Don't worry if they put some in their mouth. However, don't keep mixtures too long. Throw them away after use, and make some more.

Another idea: Add scented herbs (mint, oregano) to a pastry mix or dough.

Ready for more?

Offer a simple implement (a plastic brick, a small ball or a reel) to bash with.

Provide pastry moulds and plastic tools for your child to experiment with.

What is your child learning?

Young children learn through touch, so allowing them to experiment like this is important. The more you talk about what you are doing, the better they will learn to apply language to actions.

Strings 'n' things
making a feely string

What is your child learning?

What you need:

- *laces, or short lengths of wool, string, ribbon or cord*
- *things to thread on the strings – e.g. big buttons, beads, reels, sliced up card tubes*

WHAT TO DO:

1. Make some strings of things. Put one sort of thing on each string – i.e. buttons on one, beads on another. Work where your baby can watch you, and talk about what you are doing.

2. Put three or four of the strings in front of your baby – perhaps a string of beads, a piece of chain, a few ribbons.

3. Watch to see what your baby does. Talk quietly as they work, encouraging them and commentating on what they are doing. Help if they need it (they probably won't!) but stay near them and watch what's going on.

Another idea: Try ribbons and strings of different colours. See which your baby prefers.

Babies and young children love collections of things to play with. These strings of things will promote hand control and wrist movements. They will also encourage exploring and using language.

Ready for more?

Introduce some tins without lids (clean, and with no sharp edges). Sitting babies love dangling ribbons into the tins. If you give them light chains they'll make an interesting noise.

HELPFUL HINTS

This activity is better for sitters and crawlers than children who have learnt to stand.

Make sure the strings aren't too long. The child should be able to hold them up by one end.

DID YOU
KNOW?
Developing fine
motor control of hand
and wrist is essential
for learning to
manipulate
objects.

Let's dance
feeling security, showing affection

What you need:
- *some music on a CD, radio or cassette (experiment with different sorts of music)*

Ready for more?

'Dance' with a sitting child by holding their hands and moving them in the air (this will give you a rest!).

Babies who are beginning to stand will love to dance with you holding their hands.

WHAT TO DO:

1. Pick up your baby or toddler and dance around the room with them, holding them close to your body. Hum or sing along with the music.

2. Make sure your child can see your face and make eye contact.

3. Some children love being swung high in the air in time to the music.

4. After a while sit down together and take your child's hands in yours, following the rhythm of the music as you wave or clap together.

Another idea: Wave bells, a shaker (rice in a tin will do) or a bunch of ribbons as you dance.

DID YOU KNOW?
Positive interactions with caring adults stimulate a young child's brain and improve the links between brain cells.

What is your child learning?

Music and dancing are great activities for making you both feel close, happy and secure. Developing a sense of rhythm is an important part of child development and has a big effect on learning.

HELPFUL HINTS

You can dance with a child in a buggy or a wheelchair. Some children don't like being moved rapidly. Start gently and slowly with relaxed music.

Children enjoy doing this with others. Involve a friend's child or a brother/sister.

HELPFUL HINTS

For babies and small children play the 'tipping off the hat' game face to face before trying it with the mirror.

Some babies and young children may need to be supported to help head control or balance.

What is your child learning?

The 'tipping off the hat' game will help develop prediction. Look for your child showing anticipation and excitement. Practising words and facial expressions supports communication skills.

Look who's here!
fun with mirrors

DID YOU KNOW?
Children learn to talk by hearing words over and over again, attaching them to objects, people and actions.

What you need:
- *a mirror*
- *a hat*
- *a pair of glasses or a bangle*

Ready for more?

Dab some yoghurt on your nose and encourage your child to reach towards you and explore your face.

Use a 'no tears' shampoo to make some froth on a play mirror. Rub away the bubbles to see the reflection.

WHAT TO DO:

1. Sit beside your child in front of the mirror.

2. Pull some faces in the mirror. Say or sing 'Hello' to your child. Smile and reach for the mirror. Encourage him/her to respond to the reflections, e.g. by copying, reaching towards them.

3. Put the hat on your head and then tip it off slowly, saying 'Gone'. Offer your child the hat to put back on your head or on theirs. Tip it off gently with smiles and 'Gone'.

4. Do the same with the pair of glasses or the bangle.

5. Use words and smiles to praise their responses (copying, reaching, putting on the hat and tipping it off again).

Another idea: Get hold of a small plastic play mirror and leave it where your child can find it and play with it on their own.

Smooth operator
feeling hands and faces

What you need:
- *baby lotion or perfume-free moisturiser*
- *a shallow tray or plastic container*

WHAT TO DO:

1. Put some lotion on the tray or in the container.

2. Sit beside your baby or toddler.

3. Put a finger in the lotion and feel it between your finger and thumb. Smooth some on your own hand.

4. Encourage your child to touch and feel the lotion. With one finger, gently put a little lotion on her/his hand or cheek. Spread it out, massaging it into the skin. Talk about what you are doing. This will help them to understand what they are feeling,

5. Then encourage him/her to spread lotion on your hand or arm. Talk about how nice it feels.

Another idea: You can also do this at change time or after a bath.

DID YOU KNOW?
Close contact will now have a positive effect on personal relationships later in life.

Ready for more?

Use perfumed massage oils instead of lotion (choose mild scents and reputable brands).

Play together at bathing and then putting lotion on a baby doll.

What is your child learning?

Like baby massage, this activity will help bond the relationship between you and your child. It also helps with the idea of taking turns. Naming and describing feelings and impressions will develop vocabulary.

HELPFUL HINTS

Some children find any sort of massage very relaxing and may drop off! Make sure they are safely supported, particularly if they are very young.

Talk all the time about what you are doing and what they might be feeling. Use words like 'soft', 'smooth', 'gentle' and name the parts of the body being massaged – arm, hand, finger, cheek, etc.

DID YOU KNOW?

Developing fine motor control of hand and wrist is essential for learning to manipule objects.

Splashing out
grabbing, feeling and letting go

What you need:
- *small sponges*
- *a flannel*
- *lukewarm water*
- *a plastic tray*

Ready for more?

Put the sponges and flannel in an empty plastic food box (e.g. from ice cream), and help your baby to lift them from the box, squeeze and then release.

WHAT TO DO:

This activity works well in the bath.

1. Soak the sponges and the flannel in warm water.

2. Sit opposite your baby or toddler and offer the sponges one at a time.

3. Encourage them to grab the sponge, squeeze it and then drop it onto the tray.

4. Play alongside your baby, squeezing and dropping the sponge onto the tray.

5. Share the fun with smiles and say, 'Drip, drip', and then when the sponge has been dropped, say and gesture, 'Gone'.

6. Do the same with the flannel.

Another idea: Add some 'no tears' shampoo to the warm water and make bubbles.

What is your child learning?

Gripping and holding have to be learnt. Picking up and releasing the sponges and flannel will encourage fine control of fingers and thumbs.

Look there
distance pointing

What you need:
- *soft toys (teddy, dog, rabbit, monkey, etc.) and/or dolls*
- *a selection of suitable objects – e.g. hat, cup, flannel, mobile phone*

WHAT TO DO:

1. 'Hide' the soft toys around the room. Make sure they can be seen (e.g. peeking out behind furniture).

2. Hold up one of the objects (e.g. the hat) and give it to your child. Ask 'Who's hat is this?' 'Is it Teddy's?'

3. Encourage your child to point towards the teddy (or whichever soft toy you chose) and then to put the hat on the toy.

4. Continue playing the game, pointing to and choosing a soft toy to give a drink, wash their face, speak on the phone and so on.

Another idea: Hide cars, buses and similar toys around the room. Play 'Where's the red car?', encouraging your child to point to the correct toy.

Ready for more?

Play with a teddy and a doll identifying body parts (e.g. 'Where's Teddy's nose?' 'Where's the rabbit's tail?').

Put everyday objects in a water tray to point to, name and use.

What is your child learning?

This activity will help in combining words and gestures, which is important for communicating. It will also develop using words to name objects and describe actions.

HELPFUL HINTS

If your child finds distance pointing difficult, practise plenty of touch pointing first.

Use pointing and natural gesture regularly as you talk to your baby or young child (e.g. when you're out and about).

DID YOU KNOW?
There are lots of websites with collections of excellent counting games and action rhymes.

1-2-3, Clap with me
a counting song

What you need:

No equipment is needed for this activity. All you need is this rhyme:

1-2-3, clap with me,
1-2-3, tap your knee,
1-2-3, clap some more,
On your head and on
  the floor.

Ready for more?

Vary the rhyme by doing tiny or huge clapping or tapping actions, perhaps whisper the rhyme or use a funny voice.

Put a few toys in a box. Count 1-2-3 and tip them out.

WHAT TO DO:

1. Sit opposite your baby or toddler, on the floor.

2. Say or sing the rhyme and do the actions. Clap your hands and tap your knees, three times to the rhythm of the lines, and finish up by tapping on the floor.

3. Pause at the end of the rhyme and ask 'again?' Wait for a look, gesture (such as smiling or waving), a sound or first word intended as a request to do the rhyme again.

4. Encourage your child to copy your actions. Stop frequently to grab their attention.

5. Give lots of smiles and praise when your child joins in.

   Another idea: Take a teddy bear (or doll) and do the rhyme with his paws (hands).

What is your child learning?

This activity helps your child with first number words and with linking words to actions. Imitating, anticipating and following routines support the development of self-confidence.

Under and over
hiding and finding

What you need:

- *a small blanket or piece of soft cloth (a clean tea towel will do)*
- *objects with different textures – soft, hard, bumpy, smooth, etc.*

WHAT TO DO:

1. Sit on the floor with your baby or toddler.

2. Put one of the objects on the floor and name it as you do so (wave it gently if you need to get his/her attention).

3. Cover the object with the blanket, saying what you are doing: 'I'm covering the teddy. Where has he gone?'

4. Now encourage your child to reach under the cloth for the toy or object, or grab the cloth and pull it off.

5. Encourage and praise their efforts.

6. Try the game again with a different toy or object

Another idea: Use a toy that makes a noise, moves or plays music. Wind it up and put it under the blanket.

Ready for more?

Put the blanket over your head, gradually pull it down and say 'Boo!' If your child enjoys this, put the blanket over their head and help them to pull it off. Standing babies and toddlers will love this!

What is your child learning?

This is a co-operative game, so it contributes to the development of ideas of sharing and taking turns. Describing what's going on and naming the objects helps with vocabulary.

HELPFUL HINTS

Make sure your child is watching what you are doing. Stop and recapture their attention if they seem to be drifting.

They may need help, guiding their hand or pulling off the cloth to reveal the toy.

What is your child learning?

This activity helps with ideas of consequence and order. Listen for the sounds or words your child uses. Praise new vocabulary, or copying the words you use.

Hello, goodbye
greetings and farewells

DID YOU KNOW?
Saying 'hello' and 'goodbye' are good ways of helping your child to feel secure.

What you need:
- a few play people, small soft toys, plastic animals
- a box (cardboard's fine)
- a square scarf or piece of material

WHAT TO DO:

1. Before you start, put a few of the play people, toys, etc. in the box. If it has a lid close it, or cover it with the scarf.

2. Sit with your child in your lap or close beside to you.

3. Take the toys out of the box one at a time. As each one appears say 'Hello bear', 'Hello firefighter', etc.

4. When all the toys are out of the box, play together with them for a while.

5. When you judge the time is right take one of the toys, say 'Bye, bye bear' and put it back in the box.

6. Encourage your child to copy you as you put the toys back one at a time.

Another idea: Play with the scarf by putting it over your head or your child's head and removing it slowly, saying 'Hello' and 'Goodbye' as you play.

Ready for more?

Get a few photos of family and friends and play 'Hello, goodbye' with them, putting them in the box and taking them out.

Stand by the window and play 'Hello, goodbye' to birds, animals, cars, whatever you can see.

Hands together
squeezing and pulling

DID YOU
KNOW?
The connections between the neurons in the brain are electrical and water is essential for a good brain!

What you need:
- *net fabric*
- *dry sponge*
- *small, soft ball*
- *hair scrunchies*

WHAT TO DO:

1. Sit down with your child. On a settee or the floor with older children. If s/he is younger sit them in a baby chair.

2. Spread the items around, within easy reach.

3. Encourage him/her to reach for, grasp and hold each item. Play together at squeezing and pulling them. Encourage the use of two hands together, pulling and scrunching.

4. Talk about what you're doing and use words to describe the actions ('squeeze', 'pull', 'tug', 'grab', 'shake', etc.). Encourage them to join in.

Another idea: Try using some objects that make noises, such as a rattle, a sealed tin containing some dried peas, or a soft toy that squeaks when you squeeze it.

Ready for more?

If your child is still not much more than a baby, lay her/him on the floor and put one item on their tummy. Prompt them with words and tickles to reach for and grasp it with two hands, bringing the item up so they can look and feel.

What is your child learning?

This activity encourages the use of a range of techniques to explore an object – feeling, squeezing, pressing, shaking, listening. Using words to describe what you're doing will help develop vocabulary.

HELPFUL HINTS

Babies often find using two hands together difficult. Make sure they are sitting supported, so they can focus on their reaching without risking toppling over.

Allow them plenty of time to examine each object before you hide it.

A sight for a song
singing and chanting about what you can see

What you need:

- *You don't need any equipment for this activity.*

WHAT TO DO:

1. Sit with your child in a place where there are plenty of things to see – at a window, in a park, etc.

2. Begin to talk rhythmically about what you can see. Use plenty of repetition, e.g.

   I can see the postman coming up the street.
   Can you see the postman coming up the street?
   We both can see the postman coming up the street.

3. As you talk, begin to tap on your knees or clap your hands to the rhythm of your chant.

4. Now start to sing to a familiar tune about some more things you can see. Use a familiar tune, such as *Twinkle, Twinkle Little Star*. Here's an example.

   I see a blackbird in the tree.
   I see grandma's tabby cat.
   Can you see the blackbird in the tree?
   Can you see grandma's tabby cat?

5. Don't bother about trying to make the words rhyme (although you can if you feel creative!) or about keeping in tune. Just keep the song and the rhythm going.

Ready for more?

Sing or chant about a photo. It can be a picture from a magazine or one of your child's picture books or (better still) a family photo.

Introduce some other tunes. Almost all nursery rhyme tunes are suitable. *Jack and Jill, Three Blind Mice, Here We Go Round* are useful. Or you could use the tune from a current pop song.

Another idea: Your child will like repetition, so sing the song several times – s/he may start to join in.

DID YOU KNOW?

Music is a very important brain builder, and clapping or tapping makes it even more effective.

What is your child learning?

This activity focuses on two important aspects of child development: developing a sense of rhythm (which has a huge impact on learning) and observing and talking about the world around us.

DID YOU KNOW?

Children need practice in talking to somebody who isn't actually with them.

It's for you
taking turns with talking

What is your child learning?

Handling a phone and pressing the buttons is great for practising fine motor skills. Pretend calls develop the conventions and vocabulary of conversations.

What you need:

- *a phone (toy phone will do, but a real one is better – mobile, cordless or standard).*

WHAT TO DO:

1. Sit comfortably with your baby or toddler in your lap, on the floor or on a cushion.

2. Show them the telephone, and play with it, holding it to your ear and their ear, pressing the buttons. Talk about what you are doing.

3. Put the phone down. If it has a bell, use this. If not, say, 'Ring, ring'.

4. After the ring, pick up the phone and give it to your child. Say 'It's for you. It's mummy (or daddy, grandma, etc.)'. Hand them the phone and encourage them to hold it to their ear.

5. Keep passing the phone to each other and saying, 'Ring, ring, it's for you'.

6. Model talking on the phone so your child picks up what to say.

Another idea: Let your child talk to someone they know using your own mobile.

Ready for more?

Play the game near a mirror so the child can see her/himself using the phone. This will help with modelling.

Involve a neighbour's child or a brother/sister, so that the children can have a phone each to play at calling each other. If you have access to free calls or minutes let them play (under supervision) on a real phone.

A basket full of feelings

a texture treasure basket

What you need:

- a shallow basket (a basket is best but a box will do)
- a selection of natural objects with different textures – e.g. cones, shells, wooden spoons, brushes, natural sponge, wooden pegs

WHAT TO DO:

Treasure baskets are used a lot in nurseries to provide high quality sensory play, particularly for babies.

1. Collect the objects and put them in the basket. It should be reasonably full.

2. Sit with your child close to the basket. They should be sitting so they can lean comfortably on the edge and reach the objects.

3. Watch your child as s/he selects and explores the objects. Don't intervene unless they offer objects to you or otherwise involve you. Use the time to watch how your child reacts to the objects and manipulates them with his/her fingers, hands and wrists.

4. When they have been playing for a while name the objects as they pick them up, and encourage them to imitate you.

Ready for more?

Make a themed treasure basket – e.g. a collection of shiny, hard or metal objects.

Make a collection of things from the bathroom, the kitchen, the garden.

Another idea: Keep the basket fresh by removing some objects and introducing others, but don't do this too often. Your child needs time to revisit several times before you make changes.

HELPFUL HINTS

With a baby – or if you feel your child needs it – start with a small collection first (5 or 6 objects).

Until they get used to it your child may need you to guide their hand into the basket, but let them try on their own first.

DID YOU KNOW?

Feeling textures in a treasure basket is a excellent way of learning about objects.

What is your child learning?

Exploring the characteristics of objects (shapes, textures, appearance, sounds) is important in gaining knowledge and understanding of the world. Practising naming them will help develop vocabulary.

Hand in glove
making the most of hands

What you need:

* gloves and mittens – wool, leather, fabric, whatever you can collect

Ready for more?

Make a treasure basket of different kinds of gloves and mittens.

Put tiny baby mittens on teddies and dolls.

Make some handprints with warm soapy water or finger paint on a large mirror

WHAT TO DO:

1. Sit down with your baby or toddler.

2. Put a pair of mittens on your hands and play at clapping hands, stroking your face with the gloves, letting your child feel the soft fabric on his/her arms and legs.

3. Offer the mittens to the baby. Allow them plenty of time to explore. Talk to them as they play, describing what they are doing and imitating their actions. Smile and share their fun.

4. Hold your hands up for them to pat. Sing as they pat your hands, *'Let's pat hands together, pat, pat, pat'*.

5. Now do the same with leather gloves. Play *'Pat a Cake'* and other familiar clapping games.

Another idea: Try the game with household gloves.

What is your child learning?

This is an exercise in sharing and in exploring together. It will help your child learn to work with others (laying foundations for team work) as well as being important for tactile exploration.

HELPFUL HINTS

Younger (and some older) children may not have developed the fine control needed for this game. For them start with large, very easy to remove mittens.

Some babies and young children may dislike some textures. Have a choice of different textured gloves. Respect their likes and dislikes while encouraging them to join in.

What is your baby learning?

This is an active game that encourages physical development and co-ordination. Chasing and catching will help to develop confidence.

Follow that!
following a toy

What you need:

- *a wheeled toy on a string (e.g. a wooden quacking duck, a clicking crocodile, or even a skateboard with a favourite toy aboard)*

WHAT TO DO:

This game is best for early crawlers or walkers.

1. Sit next to your baby or toddler and look at the toy together.

2. Get up and start to move away, holding the string of the toy in your hand.

3. Encourage your child to follow you. Talk to them about what is happening.

4. Go slowly, and at first let them catch the toy very quickly. Gradually make catching a little more difficult.

5. Praise effort and success. Keep playing the game as long as they are interested.

Another idea: Play the game with a string and a bunch of bells, a shiny toy, a puppet, a few ribbons, some crinkly paper or a couple of plastic bangles.

Ready for more?

Toddlers love chasing. Tuck a ribbon or a furry 'tail' in your waistband and let them chase you!

Put wind-up water toys in the bath and see if they can catch them.

DID YOU KNOW?

Following objects helps your child to focus and concentrate as they move.

What is your child learning?

Children learn by imitating the actions of adults and the sounds they make. Grasping and releasing develop hand control. Filling up and tipping out will help them learn about the properties of objects, including containers.

In, out, tip it all out
filling and emptying

DID YOU
KNOW?
Repeating an action over and over again is called a 'schema'. Children often repeat a schema for days.

What you need:

- *ten or so everyday objects, such as a sock, a spoon, a flannel, a bowl, a teddy, plastic keys, a board book*
- *an empty plastic tub or cardboard box*

WHAT TO DO:

1. Sit opposite your child and offer them the objects one at a time to explore.

2. Show how the objects are used – e.g. wipe the flannel on your face and then gently on their face, and say, 'Look, we're washing our faces.' Encourage them to copy you.

3. Allow plenty of time to explore each object. When they seem to have finished, drop it into the tub or box.

4. Say 'Gone' as the object drops into the box. With an older child use a complete sentence – e.g. 'The spoon has gone.'

5. When all the objects have been put in the container encourage your child to tip them all out. They'll particularly enjoy this bit!

Ready for more?

Put some objects in a box and close the lid. Encourage your child to unpack the box, and talk to them about each object as they reveal it.

Another idea: Use a pillow case instead of a box.

What is your child learning?

Communicating choices is an important life skill. This activity will help your child learn to indicate their needs and wants. Using the toy's names also contributes to language development.

Fetch
pointing and vocalising

What you need:

- *soft toys – teddy, dog, rabbit, monkey, etc. (pick your child's favourites)*

WHAT TO DO:

1. Sit down with your baby or toddler on the floor.

2. Set out two or three toys, too far away for the child to reach but close enough to still be part of the game (a small mat might be helpful to make a visual boundary for the game).

3. Look at the toys and talk to your child about them. Name them together.

4. Ask your child to choose one. Get them to point to a toy they want. Older babies may be able to name the toy if it is a favourite.

5. Praise them for pointing and/or vocalising.

6. Pass them the toy and let them play with it for a while before asking if they want another toy.

Another idea: Put out different coloured plastic cups or plates for them to choose.

Ready for more?

Try the game with drinks, snacks, paint colours, etc. to encourage pointing and vocalising.

With older children reverse the tasks. You point or name, they find the object.

DID YOU
KNOW?
*Saying the name
reinforces the link in
your child's brain
between the object
and the word.*

DID YOU KNOW?

Matching similar objects helps children to group things that may not look the same but have the same name.

Two's company
matching and pairing objects

What you need:
- *pairs of objects: two spoons, two flannels, two socks, two books, two toy cars, two cups, two small balls, etc.*
- *a shallow box or tray*

Ready for more?

Put the pairs of objects in a box with a lid (a shoe box would be ideal). Shake it up, open it and sort the items into their pairs.

Put one of each pair aside and its twin in a pillow case. Hold up an object and ask your child to find its twin from the pillow case, without looking.

WHAT TO DO:

1. Put two pairs of objects (i.e. four things) in the box.

2. Allow your baby or toddler plenty of time to explore the objects.

3. Hold out your hand and invite them to give you an object. Demonstrate how it is used, e.g. pretending to eat with the spoon or to put on the sock.

4. Offer the object back to your child.

5. Play together, exploring the objects. Use single words to name the objects. Comment on the matching pairs by holding or pointing to both, saying '(name) look, they're the same.'

6. Add more objects to the box or tray. Enjoy exploring the objects together, finding matching pairs, naming objects and demonstrating how they're used through simple pretend play.

Another idea: Your child will love to tip out the box and fill it up again.

What is your child learning?

This promotes understanding of the uses and properties of objects. Naming the objects extends vocabulary.

Material world
in and out

What you need:

- *several squares of fabric, or scarves (try to find different textures, thicknesses, some opaque and some transparent)*
- *empty boxes and tubes, e.g. card or plastic tubes, cereal boxes*

Ready for more?

Play filling and tipping small boxes into a larger box.

Try shells, twigs and cones in small buckets.

Poke ribbons or wool into, through and out of small cups and cardboard tubes

WHAT TO DO:

1. Sit next to your baby or toddler and put the fabric squares between you.

2. Explore the fabric together, blowing, scrunching, wafting, folding and so on.

3. Feel the fabric on cheeks, fingers, arms, legs and toes. Enjoy the sensations together.

4. Talk all the time about what you are doing, using simple words to describe the fabrics and how they feel. Try to include 'more', 'gone' and 'again'.

5. Bring out the boxes and tubes and push the fabrics into them together. Encourage your child to try to put the fabric in the boxes, pushing and prodding, squeezing and scrunching. Pull the fabric out together.

Another idea: To make a change try wrapping paper, tissue, cellophane or foil.

What is your child learning?

This activity helps with the skills of observation and investigation and leads to the development of early concepts of shape and position. It's also good for helping to extend the span of attention.

HELPFUL HINTS

Do the same activity with noisy toys, such as rattles and shakers, and a large sweet or biscuit tin.

Play 'in and out' in the bath putting objects into and taking them out of the water.

DID YOU KNOW?

Each game of hide and seek forms and strengthens thousands of connections between brain cells.

Hide and seek
covering and uncovering

What you need:

- a soft, thin blanket or piece of fabric (not too big)
- a toy that makes a sound (e.g. a fire engine with a siren, a musical box or top, a toy phone with a bell)

Ready for more?

Put the toy right under the blanket and help your child to pull the blanket off. More adventurous children may be brave enough to go under the blanket to fetch it, but don't force this.

WHAT TO DO:

1. Sit on the floor with your baby or toddler.

2. Show them the toy and let them feel it. Play its sound.

3. Put the toy on the floor (still making the sound) and just cover it with the edge of the blanket. Keep it where your child can easily reach it.

4. Say, 'Where's the ..... gone?' Encourage your child to pull the fabric off the toy. Help them if they need it.

5. Repeat the game again. Stop when they have had enough.

Another idea: Put the object in or under a box, so your child has to lift the box or the lid.

What is your child learning?

The concept that something might still be there even when it can't be seen ('permanence') is a difficult one. This game will help its development. Reaching and uncovering aids physical development and fosters a sense of control (important for self-confidence).

What is your child learning?

This activity will help your child learn to combine words, sounds and gestures to describe actions and to make requests.

Hey-ho, here we go!
active play and gestures

DID YOU KNOW?
Repetition of songs, rhymes, actions and words strengthens the connections between brain cells.

What you need:

- a strong cardboard box
- a teddy, doll or favourite soft toy
- a bag, a hat, some keys

WHAT TO DO:

1. Sit teddy (or the doll or toy) in the cardboard box

2. Sing to the tune of *The Wheels on the Bus*, *'Teddy on the bus goes brrm, brrm, brrm... all day long'*. Encourage your child to join in.

3. Invite your child to choose another toy or doll to go for a ride on the bus. Sing, *'Dolly (or toy's name) on the bus goes bounce, bounce, bounce ... all day long'*, and gently bounce the box up and down.

4. Give the child the hat and say, *'Let's put the hat on teddy'*. Sing the teddy verse again. Repeat with the keys and the bag.

5. Use short phrases, pointing and other gestures to help the child's emerging understanding of words, objects and actions.

Another idea: If the box is big and strong enough, help your child into the box and wobble the box as you sing *'(Child's name) in the bus goes wobble, wobble, wobble...'*.

Ready for more?

Spread out some everyday objects (comb, pen, book, cup, TV remote, etc.). Name one and ask your child to find it and give it to teddy or dolly.

Make up some songs about the toys and their journey in the bus/box.

What a looker!
more mirror fun

What you need:
- a collection of hats (e.g. sunhats, floppy hats, helmets, swim hats, etc.)
- sunglasses, headscarves, hair ribbons, bows, scrunchies, bands
- a jewellery box with necklaces and bracelets
- a large mirror

WHAT TO DO:

1. Set this game up where you and your child can see yourselves and each other in the mirror.

2. Play alongside your baby or toddler, allowing plenty of time for uninterrupted, unhurried exploration and play.

3. Talk to them about the different accessories and how they look.

4. Try some of the items on yourself. Encourage your child to do the same and to choose items for you.

5. Talk all the time about what you are both doing.

Another idea: Add purses, plastic money, envelopes, a brief case, keys, a handbag or shopper for more pretend play and dressing up fun.

DID YOU KNOW?
Social interactions with you and others helps your child to process information and to reason.

Ready for more?
Your baby or toddler will love unpacking your handbag and trying out the contents. An older child may pretend to be you!

Can you get hold of a wig? If you can it will add extra fun.

What is your child learning?

This is another activity which promotes choosing and naming. In addition, experimenting with these objects will help your child to process their observations of adult behaviour.

HELPFUL HINTS

Make sure all the items are easy enough to be managed by small fingers.

Boys as well as girls will enjoy this activity. Gender is not significant at this age, so don't worry if your son dresses up as a girl (or vice versa).

You and me
simple pretend play

What you need:

- a selection of real kitchen objects (e.g. a plastic mug, wooden spoon, metal saucepan, plastic whisk, metal teaspoon, plastic plate and bowl, etc.)
- bag or bowl

WHAT TO DO:

1. Make a pile of the objects and allow plenty of time for your baby or toddler to explore them.

2. Sit with them, talking about the objects and showing what they do; for example, pretend to whisk eggs in the bowl, or to stir food in the pan.

3. Take turns putting the objects into the bag, one at a time until they've all been gathered.

4. Shake the bag and invite your child to choose an item. Say '(Name), look. You chose the...' Pretend to use the item they've chosen, e.g. 'drink' from the mug, stir with the spoon.

5. Continue taking the items out of the bag or bowl one at a time and play at using them.

Another idea: For a change try some simple in and out play, emptying and filling the bag.

Ready for more?

Play this game with a selection of bathroom objects, e.g. toothbrush, comb, sponge, towel and flannel.

Keep a basket of real objects for exploring, filling, emptying, or pretend play.

What is your child learning?

This activity will help your child to understand what different items are for and to practise using them. It will also stimulate pointing and naming.

HELPFUL HINTS

Some babies and children will need lots of practice imitating simple pretend play. Stick to just one or two very simple actions at a time.

Humour will help to keep attention on the play; e.g. drop the cup and say, 'Oh no! The drink is spilt,' and hand your child a cloth to pretend to mop up.

What is your child learning?

Learning to choose is important to your child's developing brain. By indicating control it also develops confidence. Sharing books is essential preparation for reading.

Choose me a story
sharing a familiar book

DID YOU KNOW?
Reading stories and sharing books with your child will help them to learn to read for themselves.

What you need:
- *three or four favourite story books*

WHAT TO DO:

1. Collect the books and sit down with your toddler in a comfortable place.

2. Look at the books together. Invite your child to choose one for you to tell. Concentrate on talking about the books and letting your child have a real choice. Praise vocalisation, looking closely and making choices (even if they're communicated simply by pointing).

Ready for more?
Children love repetition. You can follow this activity again and again, using the same books and introducing new ones.

3. Share the book together, stopping to point to and talk about its contents, asking your child to point to characters and objects (and name them if they can).

4. If they are still interested, let them choose and share another book.

Another idea: Let them choose a rhyme from a simple nursery rhyme book.

DID YOU KNOW?
Water has a great calming influence, playing with water releases calming chemicals in the brain.

Splash or drizzle?
making choices

What you need:
- *a small sponge*
- *a flannel or cloth*
- *warm water*
- *a small, shallow plastic box of tray*

Ready for more?

Use a tin lid or metal tray. The water will make a great sound as it hits the metal!

This is a good game for outside in the summer. Have wet cloths and sponges in a bucket for your child to wring out, splashing or drizzling on to a path or patio.

WHAT TO DO:

1. Place a few centimetres of warm water in the tray. Give your baby or toddler the dry sponge to feel. Encourage them to use two hands to reach, pat, grasp and squeeze the sponge.

2. Drop the sponge in the warm water. Play at squeezing the warm water over your child's fingers.

3. Give them the dry flannel. Scrunch it up in a ball and encourage them to poke, prod and squeeze it.

4. After a moment take the flannel back, dip it in the water and then offer a choice. Say 'Which one?' holding up the flannel and the sponge for your child to choose what they want.

5. Continue playing, offering choices and having fun splashing and drizzling the water.

Another idea: Add a few drops of bubble bath or food colouring to the water.

What is your child learning?

As well as practising choices, this is a good activity for developing fine motor skills – grasping, holding, squeezing.

Catch this
passing to and fro

What is your child learning?

An important aspect of this activity is for your child to understand your 'give me' gestures and the simple words and phrases you will be using. Naming and identifying the objects will develop language.

What you need:

- a collection of small, familiar objects in a box or basket (a treasure basket)

WHAT TO DO:

1. Sit opposite your baby or toddler.

2. Choose an object from the basket. Offer it to your child and encourage them to take hold of it.

3. Hold out your hand for the object and say, 'Give the ... to me, please.' Encourage your child by touching the object to attract their attention. Wait to see if they give it to you. Praise them if they do – smile and say 'Well done, you gave me the .... Thank you.'

4. If your child doesn't give you the object, touch it gently again and see if they release it. Use your judgement to decide whether to gently take the object back and play the game again, or to try again another time.

Another idea: Try holding out another box or a tin for your child to put the object in.

Ready for more?

If you can, get together with another parent/carer and their child. Sit in a group and pass the objects around, one to another. Young children find this difficult, so give lots of encouragement and praise them when they manage it.

DID YOU KNOW?

Learning a new move needs new connections between the brain and the body. Repeating moves strengthens links.

HELPFUL HINTS

If your child finds this activity difficult, start by putting a few objects in front of him/her and encourage them to pick these up and pass them to you.

Try passing your child plates and cups for food and drinks, etc. Then ask them to pass them back when they have finished.

My hat!
practising 'give me' gestures

What you need:
- *several hats (the wilder the better! large floppy silly hats are great)*
- *a mirror*

Ready for more?

Play this game with large plastic bangles, putting them on and then shaking them off.

WHAT TO DO:

1. Sit down somewhere with your baby or toddler.

2. Put the hats in a heap and explore them together. Put the hats on and play at tipping or pulling them off.

3. Next put all the hats away except one. Give this hat to your child and ask her/him to put it on *your* head. Prompt them with natural gestures and single words.

4. Say 'Ready, steady, go!' and shake your head vigorously so the hat falls off! When your child retrieves the hat, use an outstretched hand and words to ask them to hand you the hat.

5. Play again, this time putting the hat on your child's head. Show them their reflection, before doing 'Ready, steady, go!' to start them pulling or tipping the hat off.

Another idea: Make up a song to go with putting the hat on and shaking it off.

What is your child learning?

Children need lots of repetitive games because they focus on anticipation and prediction. Being able to predict consequences is an important life skill.

HELPFUL HINTS

This can be a lively game! Make sure there is a soft landing if your toddler falls over as they reach for things or tip the hat.

Use pointing and natural gesture to support understanding.

What's that?
exploring everyday objects

What you need:
- *some small boxes and bags*
- *several everyday objects, e.g. a cup, spoon, flannel, brush, shoe, sock, etc.*

Ready for more?

Get hold of two examples of each object. Put them in different bags/boxes and hunt for pairs.

WHAT TO DO:

1. Place two or three of the objects in each box or bag.

2. Sit somewhere with your toddler.

3. Play together exploring the boxes and bags. Name each object but also talk about how it feels, looks and how you use it. Use simple single words and two or three word phrases. Use lots of natural gesture.

4. Demonstrate the use of the object, such as pretending to brush your hair with the brush and so on. Invite your child to copy your actions.

5. Allow plenty of time for unhurried, uninterrupted exploration.

Another idea: Play again, choosing some objects that are less familiar to your child, such as a key, pen, gloves, nailbrush, egg cup, whisk and so on.

DID YOU KNOW?

Children who experience and understand simple routines will feel much more confident and secure.

What is your child learning?

This activity helps with understanding objects and what they do. It promotes listening and encourages first words. It provides a starter for simple pretend play.

HELPFUL HINTS

You might need to start with just two or three objects of particular interest to your child and build up from there.

You can help your child develop an understanding of routines by giving them an object such as a spoon to hold just before a meal, or perhaps their coat to feel just they go out.

What is your child learning?

This activity will help your child practise using fingers, fists, palms and wrists as they work. This is important in developing the hand control they will later need for writing.

Saucy!
simple food play

What you need:

- *tomato ketchup or pasta sauce*
- *a table top, or baby chair with a tray*

This gets messy, so you might want to put some floor covering down!

Ready for more?

Let your child make patterns on a large sheet of paper (remnants of wall paper rolls are ideal for this).

WHAT TO DO:

1. It is easier if your toddler is in a high chair, but you could just let them stand at the table. Make sure s/he is well covered with a big bib or apron.

2. Squeeze or spoon some tomato ketchup or pasta sauce on to the tray in front of them. Let them watch you do this.

3. Start experimenting with the ketchup, spreading, smearing, poking and patting it on the surface. Encourage them to join in.

4. Work alongside them, modelling how you can use one finger to spread, poke and make marks in the ketchup.

5. Try making some hand prints.

Another idea: Try the same activity with smooth, soft, mashed potato.

DID YOU KNOW?

Providing a rich environment which offers lots of sensory experiences stimulates brain growth.

In a hole
starting on threading

DID YOU KNOW? Connections between neurons in the brain that combine sight and fine motor skills help hand/eye coordination.

What you need:
- the post from a stacking toy (if you don't have one, use a kitchen towel holder)
- bangles, hair scrunchies, anything with a large hole in it
- lengths of ribbon or wool

WHAT TO DO:

1. Tie the lengths of ribbon or wool to make circles or loops.

2. Sit on the floor opposite your baby or toddler and put all the bangles, scrunchies and ribbon bracelets between you.

3. Explore these together, rolling, spinning, tapping, feeling, smelling and peeking though.

4. Put the bangles on your wrist for your child to pull off. Encourage them to try them on their own hands.

5. Place the bangles and other items over the stacking toy post. Drop them on one at a time and take turns with your child to take them off, all together or one at a time.

Another idea: Hold a wooden spoon so your child can thread the bangles and other things on the handle.

Ready for more?

Play a taking turns game, taking turns to choose an item and drop it on the post.

Try putting socks on each other's hands and pulling them off again.

What is your child learning?

Threading and unthreading the items is a problem, and solving it requires your child to think and act on their thoughts. It also helps the development of fine motor skills.

HELPFUL HINTS

Some babies and children find using two hands together difficult. Make sure that if they need it they are well supported, so they can focus on reaching.

As an outdoor alternative, try a bigger version of the game, placing quoits over play traffic cones or posts hammered into a lawn.

What is your child learning?

Standing up for this activity will help develop the sense of balance. Painting is a good introduction to early mark making and a stepping stone towards writing.

Paint it!
exploring paint on a vertical surface

DID YOU KNOW?
Children need to develop shoulder and arm muscles before they can use their wrist and hand muscles properly.

What you need:
- *some plastic sheeting (as thick as you can find)*
- *finger paint (it needs to be paint sold for children to use – don't be tempted to use decorating paint)*
- *large brushes*
- *protective (or old) clothing!*

Ready for more?

Introduce a second colour.

Offer some sponges or dabbers to use for spreading and marking.

WHAT TO DO:

This will make a mess, so you need to be in the kitchen where you can wipe the floor, or outside.

1. Pin or staple some thick plastic to a piece of board. Prop it up low down, where your toddler can reach it. It's best if it can go all the way down to the floor. The bigger the surface the better.

2. Put the paint pot on the floor. Start with a single colour. The aim of the activity is making marks and experiencing paint, not painting a masterpiece!

3. Stay with your child while s/he uses the brushes to convey some paint to the vertical surface.

4. Encourage them to use their hands as well to spread the paint out on the plastic, making marks, spreading, patting and smoothing. Talk to them about what they are doing as they work.

Another idea: 'Painting' with water is good fun.

In the box
making choices

What is your child learning?

Being able to choose is important for self-esteem and self image. Children need to learn how to choose through practice. This activity will also help with language development.

What you need:
- a large cardboard box
- a small cushion

WHAT TO DO:

1. Help your toddler to climb into the box and sit on the cushion.

2. Rock the box gently from side to side while you sing,
*Bobby Shaftoe's gone to sea,
Silver buckles on his knee,
He'll come back and marry me,
Bonny Bobby Shaftoe.*

3. Ask your child, 'Again?' Wait for a response. As well as listening for sounds, look for non-verbal signals such as a glance or body language, and then repeat the game.

4. Next, sing *Horsey, horsey, don't you stop, just let your hooves go clippity clop* and jiggle the front of the box up and down in time to the song.

5. Jiggle the front of the box and ask '*Horsey Horsey?*' Then rock the box from side to side and ask '*Bobby Shaftoe?*' Pause to allow your child to think and make their choice. As soon as they let you know they want more, sing the song again.

Another idea: Try some different songs. You could use your stereo to give some more music choices.

Ready for more?
Build choices into your daily routines (e.g. which t-shirt? which socks?).

DID YOU KNOW?
Children who have lots of early experience of singing and music will enjoy them for life.

HELPFUL HINTS
This activity is hard and your child may need to build up to it. Start by making choices between two real familiar objects ('Which cup do you want? Which book shall we look at?').

Allow plenty of uninterrupted time for your child to process the information and choose.

Bendy, stretchy
copying actions

What you need:
- *space*
- *lots of energy!*

Ready for more?

Play 'Copy Cat', copying your child's actions, such as patting or clapping, singing a song to describe the actions.

WHAT TO DO:

1. Find a clear space. If the weather is fine you could go outside.

2. Start jumping up and down and encourage your toddler to join you. Try jumping together holding hands.

3. Sit down and stretch out your legs. Tap your heels gently on the floor/ground. Sing,
   Stretch, stretch, stretch just like me
   I'm as busy as a bumble bee

4. Next lie down and stretch out your arms over your head. Sing,
   Stretch, stretch, stretch, just like me
   I'm as tall, as a tall, tall tree

5. Sit up and play the game again.

6. Now, stand up together, bend down low and sing, in a deep voice:
   Bend, bend, bend, getting very very small,
   Stretch, stretch, stretch, getting very very tall
   Bend, stretch, bend, stretch, up and down
   Bend, stretch, bend, stretch, now fall down!

Another idea: This is good fun for a group if you can find other children and adults to join in.

> **HELPFUL HINTS**
> If your child initially finds it hard to join in, start by imitating their actions and singing a commentary.
> Try using silly voices and different rhythms to grab attention.

What is your
child learning?

*This is a very
physical activity
which will help
your child to
learn about how
their body moves.
Copying and
imitating make
an important
contribution to
learning.*

DID YOU KNOW?
Speaking slowly and carefully to your child will help them to distinguish individual words.

Let's hear it for...
clapping and patting

What you need:
- *You don't need any special equipment for this activity.*

Ready for more?

Make some pat mats with different textures in zip lock bags for your child to pat and grasp.

WHAT TO DO:

1. Sit opposite your toddler on the floor, or sit together in a chair so you are facing each other.

2. Hold your hands out and see if your child offers their hands. If not, gently take their hands and clap them together, saying 'Clapping, clapping, we are clapping'.

3. If your child is enjoying it, try singing 'Pat a cake, Pat a cake, baker's man' while you gently hold their hands.

4. Hold your hands out and let your child pat their hands on yours, or get very close and let them pat their hands on your face. Praise their efforts at patting and clapping.

Another idea: A tin lid or mirror to pat on will introduce a new aspect to patting.

What is your child learning?

For a child to bring their hands together in front of them requires control – this is a key stage in their development. This physical activity is usually accompanied by sounds and first words, so plays a part in stimulating language.

First you put it in, then you get it out
play with tins and boxes

What you need:

- *some tins or boxes (wash food containers thoroughly first and smooth out any sharp edges)*
- *lengths of chain, shells, corks, bottle caps, pebbles*

Ready for more?

As a change, provide a purse and coins. Larger ones are easiest, so 2p coins are better than 1p.

WHAT TO DO:

1. Sit with your toddler during the whole of this activity. Make sure they are well balanced and can reach the objects.

2. Allow plenty of time to explore the tins and objects.

3. Most children need no instructions and will immediately begin to fill and empty the tins.

4. If they need help, just show them once, or play alongside them with your own collection of tins and objects.

5. Let your child play for as long as they want. Some children will play for a long time! Keep watching them to ensure they're safe.

Another idea: Provide some clothes pegs to clip on the edges of the tins and boxes.

What is your child learning?

This activity is good for promoting concentration. It also develops fine motor movements.

Spread it around
painting around yourself

What you need:
- large sheets of paper, card or anything that will take paint
- scissors or a sharp knife
- paint (suitable for children – not decorators paint)
- a large decorator's brush

WHAT TO DO:

This activity is messy but your child will really like it! You need to be in a place where mess doesn't matter or where the floor can be cleaned.

1. Get a large sheet of paper or card. The biggest you can find but at least 1m square. You can get two suitable sheets from a large domestic appliance box, and you can use both sides.

2. With scissors or a sharp knife roughly cut a circle 30–40cms across out of the middle of the card.

3. Sit your child in the hole, give them the brush and put the paint where they can reach it.

4. Stay with them as they explore the paint on the paper all round them. Encourage them to turn around, paint at the sides and behind them, reach out to the edge of the paper. Talk about the marks as they make them.

Another idea: Add some dabbers or more colours to choose from.

DID YOU KNOW?
Paintbrushes are among the first tools your child will use. Early experience of tools will help with school activities.

Ready for more?
You can do this outside on the patio. Just chalk a circle for your child to sit in and let them paint directly on to the flags. The rain will wash it away.

What is your child learning?

As well as being a lot of fun, this activity is good for developing hand control and spatial awareness. Children are often not aware of the space behind them, and this will encourage turning and looking around.

HELPFUL HINTS
If your child finds the brush hard to hold, tape sponge around the handle to make it thicker.
Put the sheet aside and use it again later with a different colour, or use the other side.

What is your child learning?

This activity has a sequence so playing it will help to introduce the ideas of order and of one action following another. It will also help them in learning to recognise, respond to and use words and short phrases.

Get it?
following and fetching

What you need:
- a small rolling toy, e.g. a wind-up car, a small toy with wheels, a small soft ball

Ready for more?

Play the game with a toy on a string, pulling it behind you so your child can crawl or walk and catch. Keep close, don't go too fast and stop when they are tired.

Get them to pull the toy. They'll love being chased!

WHAT TO DO:

This game is suitable for a child who is just beginning to crawl or is already on the move.

1. Collect some small wheeled or moving toys. Sit on the floor with your child. You could be outside if the weather allows.

2. Show your child the toys you have selected and look at them together.

3. Now roll the toy away from you both and say '*child's name* – Get it!' Use your child's name as you point to the moving toy.

4. As they move towards the toy, encourage them with words and gestures.

5. When your child reaches the toy, say, 'Good try! Can you bring it back?'. Praise them when they bring the toy back to you to play the game again, but don't worry if they don't! Just go and join them where they are and start again.

Another idea: Play the game with waterproof, floating toys in a water tray or in the bath!

DID YOU KNOW?

Watching moving toys and objects will strengthen the muscles in your child's eyes.

DID YOU
KNOW?
Fetching an object or article of clothing is much more difficult than just pointing or naming. Take it slowly!

What is your child learning?

Pointing can be an invaluable tool for children as they learn to communicate, so it needs to be encouraged. This activity will also help with learning and understanding words and phrases, particularly the names for parts of the body.

Dress up dolly
pointing and choosing

What you need:

- *shoes, hat, socks, gloves (baby clothes are really useful for doll dressing)*
- *a large soft toy or doll*

Ready for more?

Practise isolating index fingers by pressing and squashing single pieces of cereal.

WHAT TO DO:

1. Play at dressing and undressing the toy/doll together. Talk about each item of clothing, and your child to show you where it goes.

2. Encourage your child to touch or point to different body parts on the toy/doll. Say, 'Look, here's a hat. Where does this go?' If your child indicates by word or gesture where it goes, reward with smiles and praise. If not say, 'On dolly's head' and put it there.

3. Now take one of the items, and say 'Can you put it over there', pointing to a chair or table a metre or so away. Encourage him/her to look where you are pointing and help you put the item of clothing there. Continue until the hat, shoes, gloves and socks are all about one metre away, but in different directions.

4. Now the idea is to find all the items. Ask 'Where are the gloves?' Wait to see if your child indicates or fetches them. If help is needed point to the gloves and say, 'Gloves, let's put them on dolly.'

Another idea: Play with some other collections of objects, e.g. the things needed for a meal – spoon and fork, plate, cup.

Funny bunny
making up rhyming words

What you need:

- *a collection of small soft toys*
- *a quiet place on the carpet or on a settee*

Ready for more?

Play together with a pop-up toy or a Jack-in-the-Box, sharing the anticipation.

Encourage your toddler to play peep-bo games with you, holding their bib, towel or other object and vocalising

WHAT TO DO:

1. Sit down with your toddler and the toys.

2. Look at the toys together, picking them up and feeling them. Talk to your child about them.

3. Now choose one toy and introduce it. 'Hello (name), I'm Funny Bunny' (or Reddy Teddy, or Soggy Doggy, or Tony Pony, etc.).

4. As you introduce the toy, make it 'walk' across the carpet or settee towards your child. Keep saying the rhyming name as the toy advances. When you get to your child, make the toy tickle their tummy.

5. Repeat the game with another toy.

6. Praise responses from you child, whether they're words, noises or gestures.

Another idea: Use the rhyming talk as you and your child go through your daily routines. Don't use 'baby talk', just rhyming words and names (e.g. 'Here's a shoe for you, that will do').

What is your child learning?

Making up rhyming and fun names for things will help your child to develop their listening skills. Making up silly songs and rhymes helps children to vocalise. Sharing humour is good for bonding with your child.

HELPFUL HINTS

Encourage children to make up their own names for toys and objects.

Use pointing and natural gesture to gain their attention and encourage them to focus.

DID YOU KNOW?
The brain finds it easier to learn and remember rhymes. Pairing words that sound similar will help them to stick.

What is your child learning?

As they learn new songs and games, your child is learning to anticipate and concentrate. Watch for growing confidence in new activities.

Here I am, look at me!

swinging and singing the face

What you need:

- *some space on a carpet or other soft surface*
- *bags of energy! (This will be very popular!)*

WHAT TO DO:

1. Kneel or sit with your child standing facing you.

2. Hold them gently but firmly under their arms.

3. Lift them gently up and down, in a rhythmical way as you sing:

   Here I am, swing with me,
   Up and down again, look at me.

4. Ask 'Again?' and wait for a word, wriggle or look to indicate 'more'.

5. Repeat until they have had enough or you are exhausted.

Another idea: Play this game with your child facing you in a secure swing. Sing as you swing, then stop the swing suddenly on 'look at me'.

Ready for more?

Sing some rowing songs such as 'Row the Boat', where you have to move together as you sing.

Enjoy dancing together hand in hand or with both hands.

DID YOU KNOW?

Any activity that encourages your child to get a sense of rhythm and beat is good for other learning.

What's in a name?
playing a story

DID YOU KNOW?
Telling stories and reading to children improves their listening skills and stimulates their imagination.

What you need:
- *a basket of toy farm animals*
- *a toy figure (small doll, Playmobil figure) to act as the speaking character for your story*

Ready for more?

Put play animals and people in water, gloop, sand, etc. and play out stories with animal sound effects.

Encourage your child to make sound effects when you read stories

WHAT TO DO:

1. Tip the toy animals out on the floor or a table.

2. Spend some time playing with the animals with your child.

3. After you've played together for a while and your child has explores the animals, start to make up a story, using the toy figure as your main character. You could start by saying something like:

   'Here comes George the farmer. He's looking for his cows. He can hear them going moo, moo. Can you help him find the cows?'

4. Continue the story, introducing each of the animals in turn and helping your child to find them. S/he may also like to make the sounds of the animals, put them in their pens or cages, feed them, say goodnight, etc. as the story develops.

   Another idea: Play another story game with dinosaurs, zoo animals or TV or film characters.

What is your child learning?

Through frequent practice with this activity your child will learn to recognise animals (and other toy figures) and their names.

HELPFUL HINTS
Put all the toys in a bag and get your child to bring them out one at a time and name them.
When you feel your child is ready see if they can find a toy using two attributes – e.g. the black dog, the big cow.

Mine, mine!
making your presence felt

What is your child learning?

This activity introduces the idea of ownership (although it will take a very long time for your child to develop this). The starting point is learning to recognise themselves and other people in photographs. It also provides practice in early mark making, which is a stepping stone towards first writing.

What you need:

- *a digital camera or mobile phone to take a photograph of your child*
- *a way of getting copies of the photo (on your own printer or by taking the camera to a shop)*
- *sticky tape*
- *some large sticky labels*
- *a washable, chunky felt pen*

WHAT TO DO:

1. Get hold of 5 or 6 pictures of your child. You need a photos that show their face clearly.

2. Spend some time looking at the photos together. Make sure your child can recognise him/herself.

3. With your child, use the sticky tape to stick photos to some of his/her personal possessions – high chair, trike, bed, changing box, clothing draws, bedroom door, etc. Fix them at a height where your child will be able to see them easily.

4. Say, 'Let's write your name.' Help your child to make marks on the sticky labels with the felt pen. The aim is pretend writing, not the actual name. Stick the labels beside each of the photos.

N.B The aim is to do all these things with your child, not for them.

Another idea: If you can find some fluorescent ('day-glo') stickers your child will love them.

Ready for more?

Get your child to make some handprints and stick them with the photographs.

Attach photos of other members of the family to some of their things, e.g. mummy's handbag, daddy's coat. These aren't intended to be permanent!

HELPFUL HINTS

Really chunky markers are easiest for young children to hold, but make sure they contain washable ink!

If your child doesn't seem to be responding to this activity don't worry. They're just not ready for it yet. Put it aside and try again in a few weeks.

DID YOU
KNOW?
The first word that most children recognise and learn to write is their own first name.

This or that?
making simple choices

What is your child learning?

This is another activity that focuses on choosing. Your child needs lots of practice in making up her/his mind and expressing preferences. When they're around two you'll probably wish they weren't so definite! However, it's an important stage to go through.

What you need:

- *two simple snack items (fruit pieces, berries, carrot sticks, raisins, crackers etc.)*

WHAT TO DO:

Your toddler may not yet be able to say 'Please' and 'Thank you' but turn taking and watching others' responses develops social behaviour and a sense of occasion!

1. Put the two foods on different plates.

2. At snack time, offer your child a clear choice of food. Start with a choice of two things, and say clearly, 'Would you like apple or banana today?'

3. Accept pointing or their own words, and help their thinking by commenting on their choice, e.g. 'You would like banana, well done.'

4. Help them to take their choice and prompt by saying, 'Thank you.' This simple procedure, followed often, will help your child to understand social language as you model the way to do it.

Another idea: Giving a choice of drink will reinforce the procedure.

Ready for more?

Give a choice of books to look at together or toys to play with, always naming the choices and giving verbal prompts.

Ask them to choose an activity (e.g. 'Do you want to go to the park or play in the garden?'). Your child will find it much harder to choose activities because it requires a higher level of visualisation, so introduce this later and don't worry if they're not ready.

DID YOU
KNOW?
When your child goes to nursery or school, they will be given lots of choices. Give them plenty of practice.

Crawler explorer
tunnels and dens

What you need:
- large cardboard boxes
- a selection of small, noisy toys of different colours and textures

Ready for more?

Throw small cloths over the toys inside the tunnels so your child can peek under the cloths to find the toys.

Encourage your child to crawl through the tunnels pushing soft toys or beach balls (e.g. 'Let's take teddy through the tunnel.')

WHAT TO DO:

This activity is particularly good if your child is learning to crawl. It needs quite a lot of space.

1. Open the ends of the cardboard boxes and push the flaps inside to strengthen the sides of the boxes. Use the boxes to make simple tunnels. Check thoroughly for any staples or sharp edges.

2. Loosely fix the cardboard boxes tunnels together to make a run. Put some of the toys at different places in the tunnels.

3. Bend down with your child to look into the tunnel and explore what's in there Encourage him/her to peek inside, reach for the toy and then crawl through the tunnel, exploring the different sounds, colours and textures of the toys.

   Another idea: Play peep-bo from one end of the tunnel to another.

What is your child learning?

This is a physical activity, which will help your child develop his/her body. It's also an exercise in exploration and problem solving.

HELPFUL HINTS

Your child might not want to go into the 'tunnel' to begin with. If so, start with just one box and let them practise crawling through that first.

If your child is a reluctant crawler, tie their favourite soft toy and the end of a string and pull it slowly through the tunnel for them to follow. Help them out quickly if they show any signs of distress.

Point and poke
exploring holes

What you need:
- *things with holes – sieves, colanders, plastic tea strainers, plastic/ cardboard tubes, slotted spoons and spatulas*
- *UHT aerosol cream*

Ready for more?

Help your child to isolate their index fingers to make patterns in the cream, or to poke into the holes.

Spread 'hundreds and thousands' sugar strands on a plastic tray and play at sprinkling the tiny strands

WHAT TO DO:

This activity can be messy, so make sure that surfaces are protected!

1. Sit with your child at a table or on the floor.

2. Squeeze a small amount of cream into the colander or sieve and explore it with your baby, pushing it through the holes, feeling the different textures.

3. Pat the cream with the spoons and spatulas, adding more cream as needed.

4. Sing or chant a simple commentary, using single words and short phrases describing how you are both exploring the cream and holes, e.g. *'Pat, pat, pat,'* or *'Push it in the hole'* and *'All gone.'*

Another idea: Put some cream on your child's hands or tummy and sing *Round and Round the Garden.*

What is your child learning?

This activity will help your child to explore and understand objects and textures. Talking as you go will contribute to their language development, and you may find they start to imitate you.

HELPFUL HINTS

Some older children continue putting objects in their mouths well beyond the time that many babies and children do. Your child may be one of them. It's not wrong (children develop in different ways and at different rates), but be aware that it can happen.

As an alternative to cream, try mashed potato (don't worry about waste, the garden birds will eat it when you've finished).

What is your child learning?

This activity will support your child's growing interest in role play.

Time for a change
a changing mat game

What you need:
- *plastic straws*
- *small paper or plastic plates*
- *colour photos of faces cut from magazines*
- *glue stick, tape*

Ready for more?

Use a slip-in photo album to make a collection of faces from magazines, photos of children pulling faces, clowns, masks etc. Use the book to talk through feelings, or let your child explore it on their own.

Make up some stories using two or three of the masks.

WHAT TO DO:

As your child gets older and more mobile, changing time can be a bit of a challenge! These feelings masks may help to keep your relationships positive.

1. Make some simple masks by sticking photos on the plates. Attach a straw to each and keep them in a special tub or container near the changing area.

2. At changing time, offer the collection of masks to the child, so they can look at the faces and talk to them.

3. Sometimes, put one of the masks in front of your face and then pop out from behind it making a face with the same expression. This will probably result in much fun!

Another idea: Your child will particularly like the faces of other children, but it can be fun to try some animal faces too.

DID YOU KNOW?
Role play helps children to understand the feelings of others and empathise with them.

DID YOU
KNOW?
The bond between a child and his/her parents is called 'attachment'. It is vital for healthy development.

A family affair
your child's own treasure box

What you need:
- a basket or box
- objects of special significance to your child – their own flannel, sponge, favourite cloth book, comfort toy, your partner's or your gloves, hat, shoe, sock

Ready for more?

You can play this game over and over again, making a different collection of objects each time.

If you have a digital camera and printer, take some photographs of the objects and play at matching the photo to the object.

WHAT TO DO:

Your child may have played with a treasure basket before, particularly if they go to a care setting. This one is different – it's a collection of things personal to your child and your family.

1. Collect some objects for the basket. Ten or so will be plenty.

2. Give the objects to your child one by one to explore. Name the object and say whose it is, e.g. 'Look, Daddy's sock,' or 'Look, (name's) shoe.' Mime or demonstrate the use of each object use, e.g. by pretending to put the shoe on the child's foot.

3. Next, encourage your child to place the object in the basket. Repeat with the other objects.

Another idea: If you don't need the objects for a while, put them in a shoe box, stick your child's photo on it and use them again.

What is your child learning?

There are three main aspects to this activity: learning the names for things, learning or confirming their uses and learning to associate an object with a person. It will also help your child with the concept of 'mine' and 'somebody else's' (although this takes a long time to develop properly).